CREATIVE & PRO-ACTIVE MUSES

A CELEBRATION OF WOMEN IN THE ARTS

DR. MINAKSHI BANSAL

DEDICATION

This book is dedicated to all the women artists past, present, and future, whose voices and visions continue to challenge, enrich, and expand the horizons of our world. May your creativity shine brightly and your stories inspire generations to come.

ppp

Contents

Contents

Prayer

"Om Bhadram Karnebhih Shrinuyama Devah

Bhadram Pashyemakshabhiryajatrah

Sthirairangais Tushtuvamsastanubhih

Vyashema Devahitam Yadayuh

Svasti Na Indro Vriddhashravah

Svasti Nah Pusha Vishwavedah

Svasti Nastarkshyo Arishtanemih

Svasti No Brihaspatir Dadhatu

Om Shantih Shantih Shantih"

This mantra is a prayer for universal well-being, invoking the blessings of various deities for protection, health, and happiness. It emphasizes the importance of experiencing the auspicious through all senses and living a life aligned with divine purpose. The repetition of "Shantih" at the end signifies a deep desire for peace in the individual, the environment, and the universe at large. This mantra is often recited as a prayer for peace, prosperity, and the physical and spiritual well-being of all beings.

About The Author

This book represents the culmination of extensive research and meticulous analysis, incorporating a diverse range of sources, including numerous books, scholarly studies, and personal experiences. Additionally, I have scoured various websites to gather relevant information and data essential for the compilation of this work. I have taken every precaution to ensure the accuracy of the information presented and have diligently cited all sources to acknowledge their contributions.

From her earliest days, Minakshi was distinguished by an insatiable appetite for reading. Her literary universe was inhabited by characters and narratives that spanned ethical tales, motivational and inspirational stories, and the mythic parables imbued with life lessons. This voracious reading habit was not merely for personal edification but was driven by a desire to distill and disseminate the essence of these narratives to foster the development of students and peers alike. She was particularly captivated by the lives and teachings of historical figures and spiritual leaders such as Adi Shankaracharya, Swami Vivekananda, Dr. APJ Abdul Kalam, Mahamana Pandit Madan Mohan Malviya, Mahatma Gandhi, Sardar Vallabhai Patel, and Vinoba Bhave, among others. Their philosophies and life stories fueled her ambition to embody their ideals of resilience, selflessness, and relentless pursuit of knowledge.

Dr. Minakshi's academic and practical engagement with psychology has been equally noteworthy. As a research scholar, her focus has been on exploring the intricate tapestry of the human psyche, aiming to unlock the potential for psychological well-being and societal harmony. Her scholarly work is complemented by her active involvement in social work, where she employs her academic insights to make tangible differences in the lives of the underprivileged. Her endeavours in social work are characterized by an innovative approach that combines traditional wisdom with contemporary psychological practices to address the multifaceted challenges faced by these communities.

Her artistic talents, another facet of her diverse capabilities, are not merely a personal passion but also serve as a medium through which she communicates and connects with others. Her art, rich in symbolism and emotional depth, reflects her philosophical inquiries and social concerns, offering viewers a glimpse into the breadth of her intellect and the depth of her compassion.

In addition to her contributions to the arts and social sciences, Dr. Minakshi has embraced the healing arts of Pranic Healing, mastering the techniques developed by Master Choa Kok Sui. This practice, which focuses on the manipulation of Prana or life energy to heal the body and aura, has been both a personal journey of discovery and a means through which she extends her healing touch to others. Her proficiency in Pranic Healing is complemented by her advocacy and teaching of various forms of meditation aimed at rejuvenation, personal betterment, and the cultivation of harmony within individuals and communities alike.

Dr. Minakshi's life is a narrative of relentless pursuit, not just of personal achievement but of the upliftment and empowerment of society at large. Her diverse interests and talents—spanning the arts, literature, psychology, and the healing practices—converge on a singular path of service. She embodies the spirit of the luminaries who inspired her, channelling their legacy through her actions and teachings. Through her books, art, and social initiatives, she continues to inspire a new generation to embark on their own journeys of self-discovery, resilience, and altruism.

Her commitment to social betterment, particularly her focus on uplifting underprivileged children, reflects a deep understanding of the transformative potential of education and personal development. By integrating her knowledge of psychology, her artistic sensibilities, and her healing practices, Dr. Bansal has developed a holistic approach to social work that addresses both the immediate needs and the long-term well-being of the communities she serves.

As an author, Dr. Minakshi's writings offer a blend of inspirational insights, practical wisdom, and reflective contemplations drawn from her extensive reading and life experiences. Her books serve as a guide for those seeking to navigate the complexities of life with grace, resilience, and purpose. Through her narratives, she extends an invitation to her readers to explore the depths of their own potential and to contribute meaningfully to the collective well-being of society.

In Dr. Minakshi Bansal, we find a remarkable synthesis of the artist, the scholar, the healer, and the social activist. Her life's work stands as a beacon of hope and a source of inspiration for individuals seeking to make a difference in the world. Her story is a compelling reminder of the power of individual action, rooted in compassion and driven by a profound commitment to the betterment of humanity. Dr. Minakshi's legacy is not just in the tangible outcomes of her efforts but in the enduring spirit of inquiry, empathy, and service that she embodies.

❧❧❧

Preface

In the world of the arts, where the vibrant tapestry of human experience is woven with the threads of creativity and expression, women have historically played a pivotal yet often underrepresented role. It is with a deep sense of admiration and a passionate commitment to shedding light on these remarkable contributions that I embark on this literary journey to celebrate women in the arts. This exploration is not merely an acknowledgment of women's roles in shaping our cultural landscapes; it is a reverent nod to their resilience, innovation, and the indomitable spirit that has driven them to express, challenge, and transform the arts across generations.

The arts have long been a realm where the human spirit seeks connection to the larger questions of life, where societal norms are both reflected and challenged, and where the personal becomes universal. Within this realm, women have crafted their legacies, often against formidable odds. Their stories are woven with the dual threads of struggle against the constraints imposed by their times and the triumphs that their enduring spirits have secured. It is these stories—rich, intricate, and immensely instructive—that form the core of this exploration.

The impulse to create, to contribute to the arts, comes from a place of profound inner necessity. For many women, this impulse has been a beacon in their pursuit of artistic expression, guiding them through periods when their voices were stifled by societal prejudice and institutional barriers. Women artists, whether they are painters, sculptors, musicians, dancers, or directors, have not only had to master their chosen medium but also navigate the complexities of environments that were often less than welcoming to their endeavors.

This narrative begins with the pioneers, the early women who defied convention by claiming their space in the arts. These trailblazers, from the salons of Paris to the opera houses of Vienna, from the literary circles of London to the avant-garde performances in New York, forged paths that were as diverse as they were challenging. Their artistic journeys were often fraught with societal hurdles, yet they persisted, driven by the unyielding desire to express their artistic visions and to claim their rightful place in the annals of art history.

As we move through the 20th century and into the 21st, the landscape shifts dramatically. Technological advancements, evolving societal norms, and the relentless advocacy for women's rights have transformed the opportunities available to female artists. Yet, despite these advancements, challenges remain. The struggle for equal representation, the battle against typecasting in the arts, and the ongoing quest for financial parity are but a few of the contemporary issues that women in the arts continue to face.

In the digital age, the mediums and methods of artistic expression have expanded exponentially. Women have embraced these new opportunities, using digital platforms to bypass traditional gatekeepers and reach global audiences. The democratization of the arts through technology has opened new vistas of creativity, enabling women to explore and create in ways that were unimaginable just a few decades ago. This era of artistic abundance and accessibility has not only diversified the types of art being produced but has also provided a stage for voices that were historically marginalized.

This book is also a reflection on the transformative power of the arts in personal and societal realms. Through the narratives of women artists, we see how art can be a powerful agent of change, a tool for personal healing, and a means of societal critique. The personal stories of these artists illuminate the ways in which art intersects with and influences our perceptions of gender, identity, and power.

In celebrating these women, this book aims to inspire. It is crafted with the hope that the stories of these muses will motivate a new generation of women to see the arts as a field where they can not only participate but lead and innovate. Each story, each artist featured here, serves as a beacon for future generations, illuminating the possibilities that await when talent, passion, and determination meet the vast and ever-expanding world of the arts.

As we delve into the lives and works of these remarkable women, let us be mindful of the legacy they offer—not just to aspiring artists but to all who value the profound impact of the arts in enriching human life. Their journeys, fraught with both challenges and triumphs, remind us of the enduring power of creativity and the unassailable strength of the human spirit. This celebration is not just a historical record; it is an ongoing dialogue, a chorus of voices that invites us to reconsider the past, engage with the present, and reimagine the future of women in the arts.

Dr. Minakshi Bansal
Social Activist
Ahmedabad, Gujarat, Bharat

ONE

PIONEERS OF PAINT: THE EARLY WOMEN OF VISUAL ARTS

Throughout history, the visual arts have been a powerful medium for expression and societal reflection, yet the contributions of female artists, especially in the early periods, often remain overshadowed by their male counterparts. The narrative of women in the visual arts is not just a tale of creativity and skill but also of resilience and the relentless pursuit of recognition and equality. This essay delves into the lives, works, and enduring legacies of some of the pioneering women who have shaped the visual arts landscape from the Renaissance to the modern era.

In the Renaissance, a period marked by the rebirth of classical ideals and an explosion of artistic expression, women artists were typically barred from apprenticeships and thus from the very lifeblood of artistic development. Despite these barriers, several women managed to rise to prominence. Sofonisba Anguissola, an Italian Renaissance painter, became known for her portrait artistry, which was praised by Michelangelo and earned her a position as a court painter in Spain. Her works are characterized by their subtle yet powerful depiction of her subjects, showcasing a profound psychological depth that was rare at the time. Anguissola's success paved the way for future generations of women in art, demonstrating that skill could indeed override societal restrictions.

Moving into the Baroque period, Artemisia Gentileschi emerged as one of the most progressive and proficient painters of her era. Her canvases are often vivid and dramatic, reflecting the tumultuous Baroque spirit with a personal twist—many of her most famous works feature strong, defiant women from myth and scripture. "Judith Slaying Holofernes" is perhaps her most iconic piece, portraying the biblical heroine Judith in the act of beheading the Assyrian general Holofernes. This painting, like much of her work, is noted for its powerful expression of emotion and the dynamic interplay of light and shadow, showcasing Gentileschi's remarkable ability to convey dramatic intensity and depth. Her work not only earned her patronage from the Medici family and Charles I of England but also helped challenge the norms of what was considered appropriate subject matter for women artists.

As the world moved towards modernity, the 19th century brought with it the Impressionist movement, where women played a remarkably central role. Artists like Berthe Morisot and Mary Cassatt challenged the boundaries of artistic norms with their revolutionary techniques and subjects. Morisot's work was pivotal in defining Impressionist style, particularly her use of loose brushwork and soft, vibrant palettes to capture moments of everyday life. Cassatt, an American painter who spent much of her career in France, brought to life the intimate bonds between mothers and children, her compositions often marked by the tender interactions of her figures. Both artists not only contributed significantly to the Impressionist movement but also paved the way for the acceptance of women artists in galleries and salons, settings that had previously been dominated by men.

The turn of the 20th century witnessed even greater strides in breaking artistic boundaries, with figures like Georgia O'Keeffe coming to the fore. O'Keeffe, often celebrated as the "Mother of American modernism," is renowned for her distinct floral canvases that transform simple flowers into powerful, almost surrealistic images. Her work, characterized by a bold minimalism and a profound sense of spirituality, challenges the viewer's perceptions of scale and detail. O'Keeffe's career, marked by a fierce independence and a unique artistic vision, helped lay the groundwork for modern art in America and inspired countless other women artists to pursue their artistic passions without restraint.

The journey of women in the visual arts is rich and varied, stretching across centuries and continents. From the Renaissance through the Modernist period, women artists have continually pushed the boundaries of what is possible in art, challenging societal norms and altering the course of art history. Despite facing numerous obstacles, these women harnessed their talents to create works that not only stood out during their times but have also continued to influence art to this day. Their stories are not just of artistic endeavor but also of courage, perseverance, and the unwavering belief in one's craft. The legacies of these pioneering women continue to inspire and influence, serving as a testament to their critical role in shaping the narrative of art history.

❧❧❧

"In every stroke of the brush, there lies a bold defiance—a whisper of a woman's journey through the echoes of time, shaping art that speaks louder than words."

TWO

BEHIND THE BALLET: CHOREOGRAPHERS SHAPING THE STAGE

Ballet, with its intricate steps and fluid grace, serves as a powerful expression of human emotion and storytelling. Behind the seamless performances that audiences marvel at, choreographers play a pivotal role in crafting the movements and narratives that breathe life into each ballet. Among these creative forces, women choreographers have carved a unique path, often battling against gender stereotypes and traditional roles within the dance community to shape the stage with their innovative visions.

The history of ballet choreography, traditionally dominated by men, began to see significant contributions from women in the early 20th century. One of the first to make a mark was Bronislava Nijinska, a Russian-born choreographer who worked during the ballet's golden age in Paris. Nijinska, sister to the famed dancer Vaslav Nijinsky, brought a fresh perspective to ballet, blending the classical with modern elements, which was revolutionary at the time. Her choreography for "Les Noces" in 1923 is particularly noteworthy; it depicted a Russian peasant wedding through a series of rhythmic movements and group formations that broke away from the traditional focus on soloists. This work not only highlighted her innovative use of ensemble but also her ability to convey complex human experiences, setting a precedent for narrative depth in ballet.

As the art form evolved, so did the roles of women within it, with choreographers like Agnes de Mille and Martha Graham emerging as pioneers of American ballet and modern dance. De Mille's work in "Rodeo" (1942) and "Oklahoma!" (1943) introduced ballet techniques to Broadway, merging classical ballet with folk dance to tell American stories, thereby expanding the audience for ballet and giving it a new cultural relevance. Martha Graham, often regarded as the mother of modern dance, revolutionized dance with her technique and choreography that emphasized expressiveness and psychological depth. Her approach was grounded in the belief that dance should reveal the inner man, and her works often explored complex themes such as passion, despair, and ecstasy, which were groundbreaking for the portrayal of human emotion on the dance stage.

Moving into the late 20th century, Twyla Tharp emerged as another influential figure, known for her crossover ballets that fused classical ballet with modern dance and even elements of jazz and pop. Tharp's "Push Comes to Shove" (1976) is an excellent example of her innovative style that blends high art with popular movements, effectively bridging the gap between different dance audiences. Her work has consistently challenged dancers to push the limits of their versatility and endurance, contributing significantly to the evolution of ballet as a dynamic and inclusive art form.

In contemporary times, female choreographers continue to influence the ballet world with their creative explorations. Crystal Pite, a Canadian choreographer, has gained international acclaim for her narrative-driven works that combine classical elements with expressive, theatrical movements. Pite's "Flight Pattern" (2017) tackles themes of migration and human conflict, using a large ensemble to create powerful visual and emotional impacts, showcasing her ability to address contemporary issues through ballet.

Despite these advancements, women choreographers still face significant challenges in gaining recognition and leadership roles within the world of ballet—a field where men still predominantly hold the most prestigious positions in major companies. Yet, through persistent effort and undeniable talent, these women have not only crafted remarkable works but have also paved the way for future generations of choreographers.

The contributions of female choreographers to ballet are profound. They have expanded the boundaries of what ballet can express and who it can represent. Through their innovative works, they have challenged audiences to see ballet not just as a display of technical prowess but as a vibrant, evolving art form capable of telling complex stories and expressing deep emotions. Their legacy is one of creativity, resilience, and a redefined stage where the narratives and performances are as diverse as the choreographers themselves. The impact of these pioneering women continues to resonate, ensuring that the art of ballet remains relevant and revolutionary in its continuous evolution.

ᐳᐳᐳ

"When women sculpt, they do more than shape
materials; they mold the very perspectives through
which we view history, proving that strength can be
both delicate and profound."

THREE

SCULPTING HER STORY: WOMEN WHO MOLD THE WORLD

Sculpture, as an art form, is an ancient and enduring means of expressing human thought, creativity, and emotion, chiseled or cast in materials that stand the test of time. Within this domain, women sculptors have played a crucial role, often pushing against the boundaries of traditional expectations to mold not only tangible materials but also the very perceptions of art and artist. From the marble and bronze of the past to the mixed media of the modern era, women sculptors have consistently demonstrated that the act of sculpting is not only about forming objects but also about shaping ideas and challenging norms.

The journey of women in sculpture can be traced back to notable figures like Properzia de' Rossi, a Renaissance sculptor from Bologna, known for her intricate carvings on fruit pits and later, her marble sculptures. De' Rossi was one of the few recorded women artists of her time who competed with male contemporaries for commissions, a testament to her exceptional skills. Her work, "Joseph and Potiphar's Wife," carved in marble, stands out for its emotional depth and intricate detailing, marking her as a pioneer who challenged the gender norms of her era.

As the centuries progressed, the emergence of neoclassical sculpture provided a new platform for women artists. Among them, Camille Claudel stands out as a poignant figure in the late 19th century. Claudel's work was expressive and innovative, with sculptures like "The Waltz" embodying movement and sensuality in a way that was groundbreaking at the time. Her tumultuous personal life, including her relationship with fellow sculptor Auguste Rodin, often overshadows her contributions, yet her sculptures speak volumes about her profound artistic abilities and her determination to express her innermost feelings through clay and bronze.

The 20th century witnessed a significant evolution in the medium and message of sculpture, with women continuing to break new ground. Barbara Hepworth, an English artist, became a leading figure in the modernist movement. Her work is characterized by smooth, abstract forms often punctured or hollowed out, exploring the relationship between mass and void, interior and exterior. Hepworth's sculptures, such as "Single Form" and "Two Forms," are not just physical forms but are engagements with the space around them, reflective of her interest in human interaction and the natural world.

In America, Louise Nevelson emerged as a monumental figure in the field of sculptural art. Known for her large-scale abstract installations, Nevelson assembled found wooden objects into new, dramatic configurations, often painted in monochromatic black or white. Her sculptures transformed materials discarded by society into powerful statements of form and shadow, challenging traditional notions of sculpture and materials. Nevelson's work, such as "Sky Cathedral," is an exploration of her own identity and a commentary on the chaos and cohesion of life.

The latter part of the 20th century and the onset of the 21st century have seen the continuation of women's innovation in sculpture with artists like Yayoi Kusama and Rachel Whiteread. Kusama's sculptures, part of her broader artistic ventures into installations and immersive experiences, often feature her signature polka dots and are deeply entwined with her personal experiences with mental health. On the other hand, Whiteread uses industrial materials like plaster, concrete, and resin to cast the spaces of everyday objects, creating a form of negative space that prompts viewers to perceive the unseen. Her work, such as "House," a life-sized cast of the interior of a Victorian house, challenges the impermanence of space and the memory it holds.

Women sculptors have not only shaped the physical world with their hands but have also molded the course of art history. Through their resilience and creativity, they have questioned the very foundation of what sculpture can be — a dialogue not just with materials, but with societal norms, personal identity, and the larger world. Their contributions continue to inspire new generations of artists to see sculpture as a dynamic form of expression that transcends time and tradition. These artists have carved out their legacies, ensuring that the narrative of sculpture includes voices that are as diverse and complex as the forms they create.

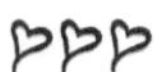

"Music produced by women resonates with the depth of their experiences, turning each note into a diary of sound that echoes the complexities of life."

FOUR

VOICES OF THE VANGUARD: FEMALE LEADERS IN MUSIC INNOVATION

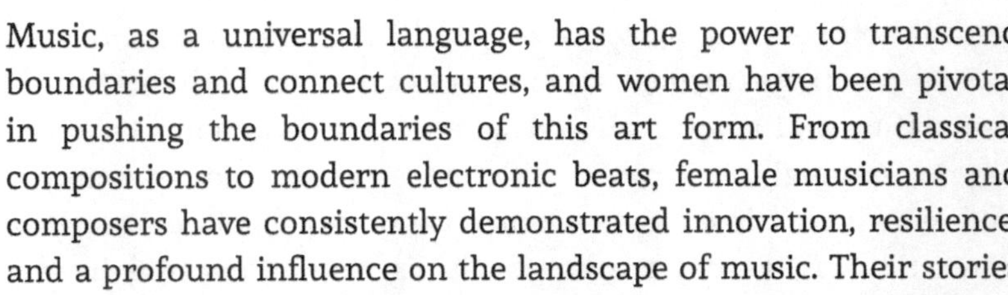

Music, as a universal language, has the power to transcend boundaries and connect cultures, and women have been pivotal in pushing the boundaries of this art form. From classical compositions to modern electronic beats, female musicians and composers have consistently demonstrated innovation, resilience, and a profound influence on the landscape of music. Their stories are not just about notes and rhythms but are interwoven with struggles for recognition and the fight to be heard in a space often dominated by men.

The journey of women in music innovation began centuries ago but found significant momentum in the Baroque period with composers like Barbara Strozzi, an Italian singer and composer. Strozzi published more secular music than any other composer of her time, and her works are characterized by their emotional depth and the complex treatment of voice and accompaniment—challenging the norms of her era and setting a precedent for future female composers. Her compositions, though often overlooked in the annals of music history, are remarkable for their expressive melodies and intricate harmonies, embodying the early signs of female defiance in the musical domain.

As the classical era dawned, women like Maria Anna Mozart, sister of Wolfgang Amadeus Mozart, emerged. Known affectionately as Nannerl, she was a prodigy in her own right, performing throughout Europe with her brother. Despite her obvious talent, societal constraints limited her career after marriage—a fate not uncommon for many women of her time. However, her early performances and the few compositions attributed to her indicate a high level of skill and creativity, suggesting what might have been had she been born in a more progressive era.

The Romantic period saw figures like Clara Schumann, who emerged not just as a muse to her husband, Robert Schumann, but as a formidable pianist and composer herself. Her concerts were critical and commercial successes, and her compositions, though less frequently performed, include works that are both technically demanding and emotionally resonant. Clara Schumann balanced her professional music career with her responsibilities as a mother and wife at a time when women were expected to prioritize domestic roles, thereby breaking social barriers and paving the way for future generations of women in music.

Moving into the 20th century, the world of music saw revolutionary changes with the advent of jazz and blues, genres where women like Billie Holiday and Ella Fitzgerald became icons not only for their musical talents but also for their resilience in the face of racial and gender prejudices. Holiday's emotive voice and unique phrasing made songs like "Strange Fruit" anthems of the civil rights movement, while Fitzgerald's mastery of scat singing showcased a technical prowess that earned her the title "The First Lady of Song."

These women did not just sing; they used their music as instruments of change, challenging societal norms and influencing the broader cultural landscape.

In the realms of rock, pop, and electronic music, female artists continued to redefine what was possible. Artists like Madonna and Björk became symbols of musical innovation and cultural icons, pushing the boundaries of music and visual presentation. Madonna's continual reinvention of her music and image challenged the industry's perceptions of female artists, while Björk's avant-garde approach to electronic music and multimedia performances has made her a pioneering figure in the genre, blending technology with traditional elements in unexpected ways.

Today, the legacy of these trailblazers is carried forward by a new generation of women who are not just musicians but also producers and sound engineers, roles that have traditionally been male-dominated. Artists like Grimes and Tokimonsta are crafting unique soundscapes that defy conventional genre labels, utilizing technology to redefine the creation and consumption of music. Their work is not just about producing sound but about creating auditory experiences that challenge the listener's perceptions of music and art.

The contributions of women to the field of music innovation are profound and varied. Through their creative endeavors, these women have not only shaped the development of various musical genres but have also challenged the societal norms that sought to confine their creativity. Their voices and visions continue to resonate across the musical landscape, proving that innovation in music is not just about new sounds but new perspectives—perspectives that challenge, inspire, and transform.

ᐅᐅᐅ

"The world of dance is enriched by the feet of women whose every step traces the struggles and triumphs of those who danced before them, and lights the path for those who will follow."

FIVE

Cinematic Shapers: Women Behind the Camera

The history of cinema is often depicted as a predominantly male endeavor, yet the influence and contributions of women behind the camera have been pivotal, albeit frequently underrepresented. Women have played crucial roles as directors, screenwriters, cinematographers, and producers, shaping the cinematic landscape with their unique perspectives and storytelling prowess. Their journey reflects not only artistic innovation but also a relentless struggle for equality and recognition in an industry often resistant to change.

The early days of cinema saw women taking on significant roles from its inception. Alice Guy-Blaché, a French filmmaker, is recognized as one of the first to direct a narrative film. Beginning her career in the late 19th century, Guy-Blaché directed, produced, and wrote over 1,000 films. Her work, which includes pioneering contributions like "The Cabbage Fairy" and "The Birth, the Life, and the Death of Christ," demonstrated early on the potential of film as a narrative medium. She experimented with techniques such as synchronized sound and color-tinting long before they became industry standards. Despite her prolific output and innovations, her contributions were largely forgotten until recent decades.

In the silent film era and beyond, other women also made their mark. Lois Weber, an American filmmaker, became known for her bold thematic choices, addressing complex social issues such as poverty, gender equality, and capital punishment. Weber's films, like "Hypocrites" and "Where Are My Children?", were controversial for their time, pushing the boundaries of what films could discuss and how they could influence public opinion.

Moving into the mid-20th century, the challenges for women in cinema persisted, but so did their determination to tell compelling stories. Ida Lupino, a British-American actress turned director, became one of the most prominent figures in Hollywood during the 1940s and 1950s. Lupino's work behind the camera was marked by her focus on hard-hitting social issues, which she explored in films like "Outrage" and "The Hitch-Hiker," making her one of the first women to direct film noir as well as issues-driven narratives.

The latter part of the 20th century and the early 21st century saw a gradual increase in recognition for women filmmakers, though disparities remained. Directors like Jane Campion and Kathryn Bigelow emerged as influential figures. Campion, with films like "The Piano," was known for her deep psychological insight and complex female protagonists. Her work not only garnered critical acclaim but also challenged the cinematic portrayal of women, offering narratives that were rich, nuanced, and profoundly human. Kathryn Bigelow made history by being the first woman to win an Academy Award for Best Director with her film "The Hurt Locker." Her directorial style, characterized by intense, fast-paced narratives, broke the glass ceiling in genres traditionally dominated by men, such as action and war movies.

In the contemporary film industry, the rise of digital technology and independent filmmaking has opened new avenues for women to create and distribute their work. Directors like Ava DuVernay and Greta Gerwig have utilized these tools to craft films that resonate with wide audiences while also addressing important social themes. DuVernay's "Selma," which portrays the historic 1965 march for voting rights, and Gerwig's "Lady Bird," a coming-of-age story about a teenage girl, exemplify how women behind the camera can influence both the form and content of contemporary cinema.

Despite these successes, the journey for women in the film industry is far from complete. They continue to face significant barriers, including lower rates of hiring, pay disparities, and limited access to major directing opportunities. However, the persistence and achievements of women in film demonstrate their indispensable role in shaping the medium. Through festivals, advocacy groups, and initiatives designed to support women filmmakers, there is a growing recognition of their contributions and a concerted effort to ensure they receive the opportunities and recognition they deserve.

Women behind the camera have not only enriched the world of film with diverse stories and perspectives but have also paved the way for future generations to continue breaking barriers. Their creativity, resilience, and vision serve as a testament to the transformative power of cinema when it truly embraces inclusivity.

ᐅᐅᐅ

"Female writers weave words into tapestries as vibrant as their lives, crafting stories that drape over our shoulders and warm us with understanding."

SIX

PEN AND POWER: WOMEN WRITERS WHO CHANGED LITERATURE

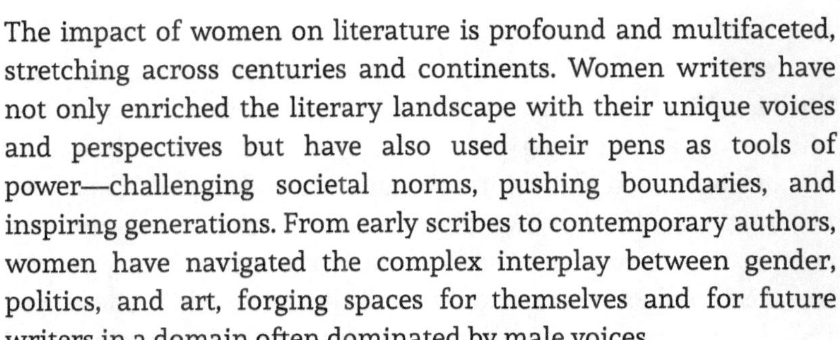

The impact of women on literature is profound and multifaceted, stretching across centuries and continents. Women writers have not only enriched the literary landscape with their unique voices and perspectives but have also used their pens as tools of power—challenging societal norms, pushing boundaries, and inspiring generations. From early scribes to contemporary authors, women have navigated the complex interplay between gender, politics, and art, forging spaces for themselves and for future writers in a domain often dominated by male voices.

One of the earliest known female writers, Enheduanna, a priestess in ancient Sumer, set a precedent as far back as the 23rd century BCE. Her hymns to the goddess Inanna are among the first examples of named authorship, signifying the beginning of an enduring legacy of women's contributions to literature. These works not only serve as religious texts but also as profound expressions of personal devotion and political acumen, showcasing the power of writing in shaping and preserving social and spiritual orders.

Moving forward to the 12th century, we encounter the writings of Hildegard von Bingen, a German Benedictine abbess whose works encompass theology, botany, and medicine. Hildegard's visionary texts, such as "Scivias" (Know the Ways), blend mystical insights with practical knowledge, illustrating the broad scope of medieval women's writing and its capacity to influence thoughts and beliefs in a male-dominated society.

The Renaissance marked a significant turn in the visibility of women in literature, with figures like Christine de Pizan. A French poet and author, Christine wrote "The Book of the City of Ladies" in 1405, a pioneering text that defended women against the misogyny prevalent in the literature of her time. Her work is considered one of the first pieces of feminist writing, utilizing the pen as a tool of resistance against the patriarchal structures of her era.

In the 19th century, the names of Mary Shelley, Jane Austen, and George Eliot (the pen name of Mary Ann Evans) dominate. Mary Shelley's "Frankenstein" is a cornerstone of Gothic literature and science fiction, raising profound questions about scientific responsibility and the nature of humanity. Austen, with her keen observations of the Georgian society, brought to life the complexities of women's lives and social standings through novels like "Pride and Prejudice" and "Emma." Eliot, meanwhile, challenged the norms of Victorian literature with her deep psychological insights and complex narratives, as seen in "Middlemarch," which explores the lives and loves of ordinary people in a small English town.

The 20th century witnessed the rise of voices like Virginia Woolf and Toni Morrison, who not only contributed masterpieces to the world of literature but also critiqued the very structures that sought to confine women's writing. Woolf's "A Room of One's Own" offers a cogent argument for both literal and figurative space for women writers within a literary tradition locked too long in patriarchy. Morrison, a Nobel Laureate, explored the intricacies of race, gender, and identity in America with novels such as "Beloved" and "Song of Solomon," providing a voice to the often silenced and marginalized.

Contemporary literature continues to be shaped by women who tackle a broad range of issues from global concerns to the intimate spheres of personal identity. Writers like Chimamanda Ngozi Adichie, with her works like "Half of a Yellow Sun" and "Americanah," explore themes of immigration, identity, and the global African experience, pushing the boundaries of how African narratives are understood and appreciated globally. Margaret Atwood's dystopian novels, particularly "The Handmaid's Tale," highlight issues of autonomy and rights, resonating with current social and political debates around the world.

The narrative of women in literature is not merely about the texts they produce but also about the ongoing struggle for space, recognition, and equality. Despite the significant strides made over centuries, women writers often still face a disparity in how their work is received and valued. However, the relentless spirit of innovation and advocacy that defines their contribution continues to inspire and effect change. Through their writings, women have not only transformed the literary world but have also wielded their pens as instruments of power, advocating for justice, equality, and human rights. The legacy of women in literature is a testament to the enduring power of the word as both an artistic expression and a vehicle for social change.

ppp

"In the realm of digital arts, women are not just participants; they are pioneering architects, building landscapes where bytes and creativity meet beneath the infinite sky of possibility."

SEVEN

THE FABRIC OF SOCIETY: WOMEN IN TEXTILE ARTS

The textile arts have long been a domain where the threads of history, culture, and individual expression are interwoven, creating a rich tapestry that reflects the lives and landscapes of its creators. Women, in particular, have played a fundamental role in the evolution of these arts, using their looms and needles not just as tools of craft but also as instruments of storytelling, resistance, and education. The contributions of women to the textile arts stretch across various cultures and epochs, showcasing a diverse array of skills and innovations that have significantly shaped both the artistic and social fabric of societies around the world.

In many cultures, the skills related to textile production—spinning yarn, weaving, sewing, and embroidery—have traditionally been passed down from mother to daughter, becoming deeply embedded in the community's daily life and cultural identity. These textile practices have provided women with a form of expression and autonomy, allowing them to embed personal and collective narratives into their fabrics. For instance, the intricate patterns woven into the kilims of Anatolia or the detailed stitch work of Japanese kimonos carry with them stories of geographical origins, tribal affiliations, and spiritual beliefs, narrated thread by thread by the hands of women.

During the medieval period in Europe, tapestries were one of the most prestigious forms of textile art, often depicting scenes from the Bible, mythology, or medieval court life. Women from affluent backgrounds were key contributors to the weaving and embroidery of these pieces. One famous example is the Bayeux Tapestry, believed to have been commissioned by Queen Matilda, wife of William the Conqueror, and possibly crafted by her and her court's ladies. This historical embroidery vividly chronicles the Norman conquest of England in 1066. Not merely decorative, these works served as narrative tools that recorded and communicated the historical and cultural values of the time.

Moving forward to the 17th and 18th centuries, quilting became a significant aspect of domestic life, particularly in colonial America where women would gather in groups to quilt. These gatherings were not only practical but also social, serving as spaces where women could share news, support each other, and collectively influence community decisions. Quilts also began to serve as historical documents, capturing significant life events and local histories through their patterns and motifs.

The 19th century marked a turning point with the Arts and Crafts Movement, which opposed the dehumanizing effects of industrial production and emphasized the value of handcrafted goods. Women like Jane Morris and May Morris in England became central figures in this movement, advocating for art that integrated beauty and utility. They helped revive traditional techniques and brought respected artistic recognition to textile arts, which had often been categorized merely as women's crafts rather than "high" art.

In the 20th century, the art world saw a radical reevaluation of the textile arts, thanks in large part to modern female artists who pushed the boundaries of these traditional mediums. Artists like Anni Albers, who fled Nazi Germany and joined the Bauhaus movement, championed textiles as a legitimate medium of artistic expression. Albers explored the structural possibilities of textiles, blending innovation with tradition, and her works helped elevate weaving beyond functional craft to a fine art form.

Contemporary textile artists continue to challenge conventional notions about craft and art. Faith Ringgold, an African American artist known for her story quilts, combines fabric, storytelling, and painting to address complex narratives about identity, race, and gender. Her works, such as "Tar Beach," not only depict personal and historical narratives but also critically engage with broader social issues, making her textiles a canvas for cultural commentary and activism.

The involvement of women in textile arts is a profound reminder of how deeply interlaced these practices are with societal transformations. Through their contributions to textile arts, women have not only preserved cultural heritage and passed on traditional knowledge but have also made space for innovation and commentary on contemporary issues. The evolution of textile arts under the hands of women is a narrative about creativity, resilience, and the enduring human desire to make and mean—where each stitch and weave is a reflection of both personal and collective identities.

ॐॐॐ

"Art therapy, guided by the gentle hands of women, stitches the fabric of the psyche back together, one colorful thread at a time, healing as it weaves."

EIGHT

THE ART OF INFLUENCE: WOMEN IN MEDIA AND PUBLIC ART

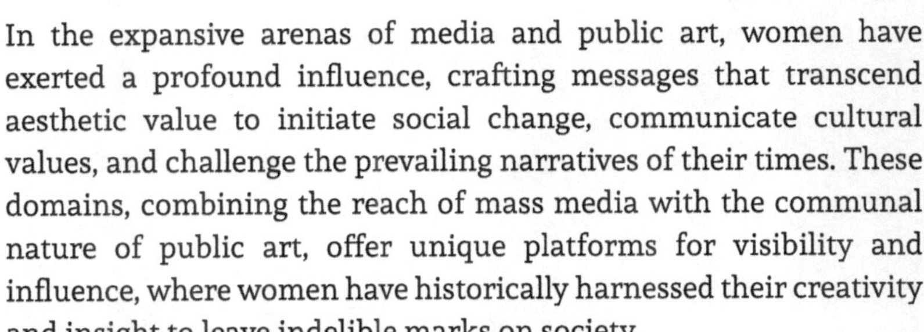

In the expansive arenas of media and public art, women have exerted a profound influence, crafting messages that transcend aesthetic value to initiate social change, communicate cultural values, and challenge the prevailing narratives of their times. These domains, combining the reach of mass media with the communal nature of public art, offer unique platforms for visibility and influence, where women have historically harnessed their creativity and insight to leave indelible marks on society.

From the early days of print media to the digital revolutions of the 21st century, women have been pivotal in shaping public opinion and articulating social issues. Pioneers like Nellie Bly in the late 19th century demonstrated the power of investigative journalism by exposing the harsh realities of mental asylum conditions in New York, using her reports as a force for significant reform. Bly's work not only expanded the scope of journalism but also showcased the potential of women in media to influence public policy and societal norms.

As the 20th century progressed, women in various forms of media continued to push boundaries. In the realm of broadcast journalism, figures such as Barbara Walters and Oprah Winfrey broke the glass ceiling, with Walters becoming the first female co-anchor of a network evening news program and Winfrey revolutionizing daytime television with her eponymous talk show. Oprah Winfrey's impact extends beyond her role as a broadcaster; she transformed her platform into a tool for education, empowerment, and social justice, tackling complex issues such as race, gender, and poverty, and encouraging open dialogue on topics often deemed taboo.

In the contemporary digital age, women have leveraged new media tools to create influential content and foster global communities. Bloggers, vloggers, and social media influencers like Malala Yousafzai utilize platforms like YouTube, Twitter, and Instagram to advocate for women's rights and education, demonstrating media's power as a vehicle for advocacy and global change. The digital realm has democratized media production and distribution, enabling women to bypass traditional gatekeepers and reach wide audiences directly.

Parallel to their impact in media, women have also been central figures in the realm of public art, which serves as a visual dialogue between the artwork and the community. Public art by women often engages with the environment and social context, offering commentary on public policies, cultural histories, and community identities. For instance, Maya Lin's Vietnam Veterans Memorial in Washington, D.C., is a poignant example of how public art can evoke collective memory and healing. Lin's design, chosen when she was just an undergraduate student, was initially controversial but ultimately acclaimed for its contemplative and non-traditional approach, which has deeply influenced how we think about monuments and memorials.

Street art, another form of public expression, has also seen significant contributions from women who use urban spaces as canvases to challenge political and social norms. Artists like Banksy have garnered much attention, yet women street artists like Swoon and Lady Pink bring unique perspectives to this traditionally male-dominated field. Their works often explore issues of gender, empowerment, and social justice, enriching the urban landscape with visually compelling imagery that prompts public reflection and dialogue.

Furthermore, in the sphere of performance art, women like Marina Abramović have used their bodies as mediums to explore and challenge perceptions of the physical and metaphysical. Abramović's performances, which often test the limits of endurance, invite public interaction and highlight the profound potential of art to influence personal and collective awareness.

The contributions of women in media and public art underscore the dynamic ways in which art and expression intersect with societal issues. Through newspapers, television, digital platforms, sculptures, murals, and performances, women have not only shaped the aesthetic dimensions of public spaces but have also crafted powerful platforms for advocacy, education, and social critique. These endeavors reflect a broader narrative of resilience and transformation, demonstrating that the act of creation is also an act of influence, with the power to challenge, redefine, and inspire societal progress.

ᗰᗰᗰ

"Experimental art by women does not just push boundaries—it redraws them, inviting us to step into realms of radical imagination and transformative power."

NINE

Harmony and Heritage: Preserving Cultural Arts

The preservation of cultural arts stands as a vital bridge between the past and present, offering future generations a window into the traditions, values, and aesthetics of their forebears. This endeavor, deeply intertwined with the identities of communities and nations, relies significantly on the dedication and creativity of individuals who understand the importance of cultural continuity and evolution.

Among these custodians, women have played a critical role, harnessing the arts to safeguard their heritage and share it with the world, ensuring that the rhythms, colors, and stories that define their cultures endure in an ever-globalizing world.

Preserving cultural arts encompasses a range of activities—from the revitalization of traditional crafts, such as weaving and pottery, to the performance arts like dance and music, to the culinary arts, each carrying distinct elements of cultural significance.

Women, often the primary transmitters of cultural knowledge within communities, have been at the forefront of these preservation efforts, infusing traditional practices with contemporary relevance and advocating for their recognition and protection.

In the realm of traditional crafts, women artisans are often seen as the keepers of ancestral wisdom. For instance, Native American women across various tribes have preserved the art of basket weaving, passing down intricate designs and techniques that are imbued with cultural and spiritual meanings. These baskets are more than utilitarian objects; they are a form of storytelling and a repository of communal history, crafted from materials that are locally sourced and spiritually significant.

Similarly, in the Andean regions of South America, indigenous women maintain the practice of textile weaving, using patterns and colors that date back to pre-Colombian times to narrate stories of their landscape, community, and beliefs.

The preservation of performance arts also sees significant contributions from women, who uphold and evolve traditional dance and music. In Bali, the legong dance, characterized by its intricate gestures and expressions, is traditionally performed by young girls who begin their training under female gurus from a very early age. These gurus not only teach the dance but also imbue their students with a deep respect for the cultural and spiritual elements that the dance represents.

In West Africa, women griots (storytellers and musicians) play a crucial role in preserving oral histories and genealogies through song, connecting current generations to their ancestral past.

Culinary arts, too, are a profound expression of cultural heritage, with recipes and techniques passed down through generations. Women, traditionally the stewards of family recipes, play a pivotal role in the conservation and sharing of culinary traditions that might otherwise be lost to time.

For example, in Italy, the art of making pasta by hand is an age-old tradition that many women continue to preserve, teaching the nuances of dough texture and shape that vary from one region to another. Through such efforts, these women ensure that the richness of their cultural gastronomy remains vibrant and relevant.

Furthermore, the role of women in the academic and institutional spheres of cultural preservation cannot be understated. Many female anthropologists, historians, and curators have dedicated their careers to the study and preservation of cultural arts.

Their work in museums, cultural centers, and universities not only helps in conserving physical artifacts and practices but also in interpreting cultural significance, offering insights that foster a deeper appreciation and understanding among the broader public.

Despite these contributions, women in the field of cultural preservation often face challenges ranging from limited recognition and funding to the undervaluation of traditional arts as mere crafts rather than expressions of profound cultural and historical significance. However, through networks of community workshops, cultural festivals, and collaborations with global preservation entities, women continue to advocate for the essential role of cultural arts in maintaining community identity and heritage.

The endeavors of women in preserving cultural arts are thus essential not only in maintaining cultural diversity but also in promoting sustainable development, as these arts provide economic opportunities and enhance social cohesion.

By ensuring that traditional arts are passed on to new generations and adapted to contemporary contexts, these women act as bridges between the old and the new, enabling their cultures to thrive in a changing world. Their work underscores the belief that the arts are a fundamental aspect of human society, necessary for understanding our past and shaping our future.

ppp

"Indigenous women artists carry the palette of their ancestors, painting the future with echoes of the past and strokes of enduring resilience."

TEN

GLASS CEILINGS AND STAINED GLASS: WOMEN IN GLASS ARTS

The world of glass arts, encompassing both the delicate craft of stained glass and the broader field of glassmaking, stands as a vivid testament to creativity and resilience. Within this sphere, women have emerged as pivotal figures, navigating and dismantling the proverbial glass ceilings that have constrained their artistic expression and professional advancement. The contributions of these women are not merely artistic—they are revolutionary acts that redefine the medium and challenge the traditional narratives within the glass art community.

Historically, the art of glassmaking has been predominantly male-dominated, rooted deeply in guilds and family lineages that often excluded women from apprenticeship opportunities. Despite these barriers, women have been involved in glass art for centuries, initially finding opportunities in the design phases or in decorative applications without receiving acknowledgment for their contributions. However, the 20th century marked a significant shift, with women artists stepping firmly into the light of recognition and innovation.

In the realm of stained glass, artists like Mary Elizabeth Tillinghast and Margaret Agnes Rope carved niches for themselves in what was a rigidly structured field. Tillinghast, an American artist active in the late 19th and early 20th centuries, was known for her formidable talent in stained glass design, which graced many prestigious buildings across the United States. Her works are characterized by their luminous quality and intricate detail, which rival the craftsmanship of any of her male contemporaries. Across the Atlantic, Margaret Agnes Rope, working in England during the same period, produced numerous stained glass windows for churches and cathedrals, imbued with vibrant colors and complex iconography, showcasing her deep religious conviction and artistic prowess.

The studio glass movement, which began in the mid-20th century, further democratized the field of glass art, allowing artists to create glass works in smaller studio settings and pushing the boundaries of glass as a medium for personal artistic expression. This movement saw the emergence of pioneering women like Dominick Labino and Harvey Littleton, who facilitated new techniques and possibilities in glassmaking that were previously unexplored. Women artists like Karen LaMonte and Toots Zynsky took these opportunities to develop distinct styles that challenged the very fabric of traditional glass art. LaMonte is celebrated for her hauntingly beautiful and ethereal cast glass sculptures that often depict dresses and drapery, void of human presence yet brimming with life. Zynsky's unique heat-formed glass threads works, which she fuses into undulating, textured vessels, display a vibrant interplay of light, color, and form, pushing the boundaries of glass as functional and decorative art.

Moreover, the expansion of glass art into multimedia and performance art has provided women artists additional avenues to explore and express complex themes. Artists like Judy Chicago, known for her contributions to feminist art, have incorporated glass in installations that tackle strong social messages, particularly those pertaining to female identity and power dynamics. Chicago's work not only utilizes the intrinsic qualities of glass to reflect and refract but also metaphorically underscores the fragility and resilience inherent in the struggle for gender equality.

Contemporary women in glass arts continue to innovate and inspire, harnessing technological advancements and interdisciplinary approaches to expand the possibilities of the medium. They engage with themes ranging from environmental issues to explorations of digital identity, ensuring that glass art remains a dynamic and relevant form of contemporary expression. The global glass community, with festivals, exhibitions, and collaborations, has become increasingly inclusive, although challenges persist in terms of representation and equity.

The narratives of women in glass arts are richly layered stories of breaking through barriers—both literal and metaphorical. Their work not only transforms raw, brittle material into objects of profound beauty and significance but also challenges the long-held perceptions of what women can achieve in the realms of art and craft. Through their persistent efforts, these artists have not only shattered ceilings but also reassembled the shards into stunning expressions of art, symbolizing both rebirth and resilience. Their legacies illuminate the paths for future generations of women artists, ensuring that the glass ceiling is not just broken but also remolded into luminous stained glass windows that open up to new horizons.

ppp

*"The canvases of female painters are not just art;
they are arenas of battle and beauty, where each
color tells a story of defiance and each line charts
the maps of change."*

ELEVEN

DIGITAL DIMENSIONS: WOMEN PIONEERS IN DIGITAL ART AND ANIMATION

The realm of digital art and animation represents a frontier of modern artistic expression, characterized by its fluidity, accessibility, and revolutionary potential. Within this evolving landscape, women pioneers have played a crucial role, not only in shaping the aesthetic and technical aspects of these mediums but also in redefining the possibilities of digital technologies in art. These artists have harnessed the power of digital tools to create works that are not only visually compelling but also rich in narrative and innovation, challenging traditional notions of art and its creation.

The advent of digital art can be traced back to the late 20th century, as computer technology began to evolve at an exponential pace. One of the earliest influencers in this space was Vera Molnár, a pioneer of computer-generated art. Born in Hungary and working primarily in France, Molnár began experimenting with algorithmic painting in the 1960s, using computers to create visual art that explored geometric abstraction through mathematical precision. Her work is notable for its systematic exploration of form and color, which she manipulated through programming to produce patterns that no human hand could precisely replicate. Molnár's contributions laid foundational concepts for the use of algorithms in art, a practice that would expand dramatically with the rise of personal computing.

As the digital revolution took hold, more women entered the field, expanding its boundaries and exploring its possibilities. Lynn Hershman Leeson, another trailblazer, explored the interactivity of digital media through art installations and cinema. Her works often addressed issues such as identity, surveillance, and the relationship between humans and technology, using interactive digital media as a tool to engage viewers in active dialogue with the art piece. Her groundbreaking installation and performance art piece, "Lorna," was one of the first interactive video art installations, allowing participants to navigate through a video narrative using a remote control, thereby prefiguring the interactive possibilities of digital technologies in multimedia art.

In the realm of animation, women have also made significant strides, using digital tools to bring diverse stories and visual styles to life. Jennifer Yuh Nelson, known for her directorial work on "Kung Fu Panda 2," stands out as a prominent figure in this field. Her direction brought a depth of character and an innovative visual style to the animated film, which became the highest-grossing film ever directed by a woman at the time of its release. Nelson's success is a testament to the critical role that women play in animation, not only in contributing to the medium's artistic evolution but also in challenging the industry's gender dynamics.

The impact of digital technology on art has also democratized the field, enabling more artists to produce and distribute their work independently. This shift has been particularly significant for women artists, who have used platforms like Instagram, YouTube, and Vimeo to circumvent traditional gatekeepers in the art and animation industries. For instance, artists like Loish (Lois van Baarle) have gained international fame through their digital artworks and tutorials shared on social media platforms, inspiring a new generation of digital artists with their distinctive styles and personal engagement with their audiences.

Moreover, women in digital arts have not only been pioneers in the aesthetic creation but also in technological innovation. Rebecca Allen, an internationally recognized media artist, has pushed the boundaries of virtual reality and artificial intelligence in art. Her work explores the fluid boundary between reality and virtual experiences, creating immersive environments that challenge our perceptions of space and identity.

Women's contributions to digital art and animation are profound and multifaceted, extending beyond their roles as creators to include educators, innovators, and leaders in the field. Their work continues to inspire not just new aesthetic values but also new ways of thinking about and interacting with the digital world. As digital technology continues to evolve, the influence of women in this field is increasingly vital, ensuring that the future of digital arts remains as diverse and dynamic as the technology itself. Their pioneering efforts not only pave the way for future generations of artists but also ensure that the digital arts remain at the forefront of cultural, technological, and artistic innovation.

ᐅᐅᐅ

"The films directed by women are windows to diverse worlds, where the lens focuses on untold stories, reframing reality with each frame captured."

TWELVE

Photographic Perspectives: Female Photographers Capturing Truths

Photography, as an art form and a tool of documentation, has the profound capacity to capture and convey truths, framing the world through the unique perspectives of those behind the lens. Female photographers, in particular, have utilized this medium to explore and express a multiplicity of realities, often challenging societal norms and revealing overlooked stories. Their work has not only enriched the field of photography but has also played a crucial role in social activism, by bringing critical issues to the public's attention and stimulating dialogue on a global scale.

The journey of women in photography began in the mid-19th century, shortly after the invention of the camera. Early pioneers like Julia Margaret Cameron, one of the first women to gain recognition in the photography world, used the medium to create intimate and profoundly expressive portraits. Cameron's approach was not merely about capturing the appearance of her subjects but rather about revealing their inner essence. Her portraits of Victorian intellectuals, artists, and even her own relatives are characterized by an unusual use of soft focus and tight framing, which were innovative for her time and demonstrated her visionary approach to photography.

As the 20th century progressed, more women began to embrace photography, not only as a form of personal expression but also as a professional endeavor. Dorothea Lange's work during the Great Depression exemplifies how photography can serve as a powerful agent for social change. Hired by the Farm Security Administration to document the impact of economic decline on American families, Lange's photographs, such as the iconic "Migrant Mother," humanized the consequences of the Great Depression and influenced the development of documentary photography. Her ability to convey the profound struggles and resilience of her subjects helped spur government action to aid those affected by the crisis.

In the realms of fashion and culture, women photographers like Diane Arbus and Vivian Maier also made significant contributions. Arbus, known for her stark black-and-white photographs, delved into the lives of those on the fringes of society — the marginalized, the overlooked, and the taboo. Her candid portrayals invited viewers to see the world through a lens that questioned the norms of beauty and normality. Vivian Maier, on the other hand, spent her life as a nanny, while secretly documenting the urban life of America with her Rolleiflex camera. Her photographs, discovered posthumously, revealed a rich tapestry of mid-century urban life and demonstrated her keen observational skills and artistry.

The late 20th and early 21st centuries saw the emergence of digital photography and the Internet, which transformed the landscape of the medium. Women photographers adapted swiftly to these changes, using digital platforms to reach global audiences. Photographers like Annie Leibovitz have become cultural icons in their own right. Leibovitz's work, known for its bold colors and dramatic compositions, captures the essence of celebrities and public figures, making her one of the most influential photographers of our time. Her portraits go beyond mere representation, offering insights into the personalities and dynamics of her subjects, thus shaping public perceptions of these individuals.

Contemporary female photographers continue to push the boundaries of the medium, exploring issues such as identity, race, and environmental concerns. For instance, LaToya Ruby Frazier's work focuses on the social and environmental injustices faced by marginalized communities in the United States. Her photographs not only document the impact of industrial decline on communities but also serve as a form of activism, aiming to bring about policy changes to address these injustices.

Through their lenses, women photographers capture more than just images; they capture truths that might otherwise remain unseen. They challenge viewers to confront uncomfortable realities and to reconsider their perspectives on beauty, truth, and justice. Their contributions go beyond the art of photography; they foster a deeper understanding and awareness among audiences worldwide. In this way, female photographers do not merely document the world as it is — they envision the world as it could be, making photography a dynamic tool for reflection, transformation, and change.

ﭘﭘﭘ

"In photography, women capture more than images;
they snapshot history, seize moments of truth, and
frame the narratives long marginalized by the
mainstream."

THIRTEEN

STAGE PRESENCE: WOMEN DIRECTORS IN THEATRE

The world of theatre has long been a reflective mirror to society, capturing the complexities of human emotions and societal dynamics through the art of performance. Within this vibrant space, women directors have carved out significant roles for themselves, utilizing the stage not just to entertain but to challenge, provoke, and reinterpret narratives. Their influence on theatre extends beyond the aesthetic to impact the broader conversations about gender, power, and representation in the arts.

Historically, theatre, like many other artistic fields, was predominantly male-dominated, with women often relegated to roles in front of the curtain rather than behind it. However, the 20th century heralded a shift, beginning a slow but steady transformation towards inclusivity. This change was propelled by pioneering women who not only claimed their space in theatre but also redefined what could be achieved through the medium.

Pioneers like Hallie Flanagan, director of the Federal Theatre

Project in the 1930s, demonstrated early on the potential of theatre to serve as a platform for social commentary and change. Under her leadership, the Federal Theatre Project not only provided employment for thousands during the Great Depression but also brought socially conscious plays to a national audience, often highlighting issues of race, poverty, and injustice. Flanagan's work laid the groundwork for the idea of theatre as an arena for public discourse, setting the stage for future generations of women directors.

In the latter half of the 20th century, the rise of feminist theatre brought new momentum to the involvement of women in directing. Visionaries like Julie Taymor and Garry Hynes broke through the theatrical glass ceiling with their bold reinterpretations of classic and contemporary texts. Taymor, known for her visually stunning and innovative productions such as "The Lion King," brought a new dimension to Broadway, blending puppetry, live acting, and intricate visuals to tell universally appealing stories. Her direction not only won her critical acclaim but also commercial success, proving that female directors could achieve and sustain massive box office appeal.

Garry Hynes, another trailblazer, became the first woman to win a Tony Award for Best Direction of a Play for her work on "The Beauty Queen of Leenane" in 1998. Hynes' directorial style, characterized by its sharpness and depth, demonstrates an acute understanding of the human condition, making her productions impactful and memorable. Her success paved the way for more women to assume leadership roles in theatre, challenging the narrative and expectations of what women could achieve in directing.

The 21st century has seen a continued expansion of women's roles in theatre direction, with more women leading major productions and gaining recognition for their unique perspectives and innovative approaches. Directors like Ivo van Hove and Pam MacKinnon have been instrumental in bringing diverse stories to the forefront, often focusing on underrepresented voices and complex social issues. Their productions frequently explore themes of identity, power, and societal structures, inviting audiences to question and reflect on their own views and biases.

Moreover, the impact of women directors extends beyond the professional sphere into the educational and developmental realms of theatre. Through workshops, mentorships, and advocacy, these women have nurtured the next generation of theatre artists, ensuring that the field not only grows in diversity but also in depth and sensitivity. They champion the idea that theatre is a powerful tool for education and transformation, capable of fostering empathy and understanding across diverse audiences.

Women directors in theatre contribute significantly to the vibrancy and relevance of the art form. Their work challenges the status quo, encourages innovation, and expands the possibilities of what theatre can achieve. By reimagining narratives and presenting new perspectives, they not only enrich the theatrical landscape but also contribute to the broader dialogue about culture, society, and the power of art. As they continue to break barriers and inspire change, their legacies will resonate both on and off the stage, affirming theatre's role as a catalyst for reflection and evolution in society.

ppp

"The crafts fashioned by women's hands are never merely objects; they are vessels of tradition, bearing the weight of cultural stories and the warmth of communal bonds."

FOURTEEN

FROM POTTERY TO POLITICS: THE SOCIOPOLITICAL IMPACT OF WOMEN'S CRAFTS

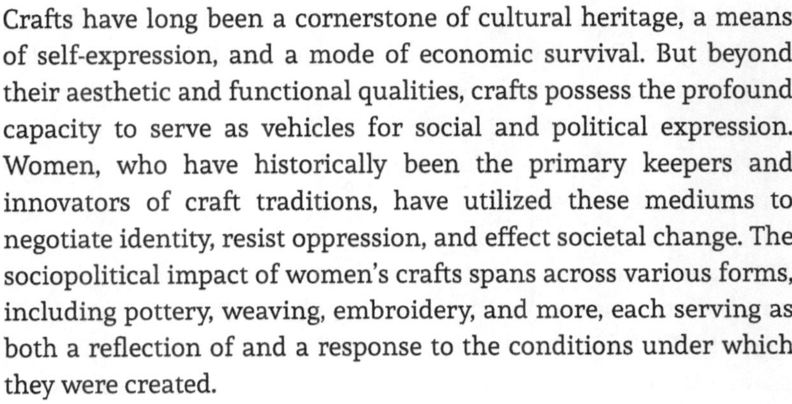

Crafts have long been a cornerstone of cultural heritage, a means of self-expression, and a mode of economic survival. But beyond their aesthetic and functional qualities, crafts possess the profound capacity to serve as vehicles for social and political expression. Women, who have historically been the primary keepers and innovators of craft traditions, have utilized these mediums to negotiate identity, resist oppression, and effect societal change. The sociopolitical impact of women's crafts spans across various forms, including pottery, weaving, embroidery, and more, each serving as both a reflection of and a response to the conditions under which they were created.

The link between women's crafts and their sociopolitical impact can be traced back through countless societies and epochs. In many cultures, the act of making—whether forming clay or stitching cloth—has been imbued with significant cultural meanings and social practices, often passed down through generations of women. These crafts are not merely decorative but are imbued with stories and symbols that communicate community values, historical events, and political messages. For instance, Native American women have used pottery and basket-weaving not only as a means of artistic expression but also as a way to preserve and assert cultural identity under the pressures of colonization and cultural assimilation.

In the American Southwest, for example, Pueblo women have been making pottery for centuries, using techniques and designs passed down from their ancestors. Each piece is not just utilitarian; it is a work of art, reflecting the cultural and spiritual life of the community. During periods of cultural repression, these pots became repositories of Pueblo culture, subtly preserving and resisting through their traditional designs and methods of creation. Similarly, the Gee's Bend quilts, made by generations of African American women in Alabama, are celebrated not only for their bold colors and patterns but also for their rich historical narratives and their role in the civil rights movement. These quilts, which were originally crafted from scraps of old clothing and other textiles, reflect the resilience and creativity of the women who made them. They served as literal and metaphorical banners for the civil rights movement, with some being used as fund-raisers to support the struggle for racial equality.

Embroidery and textile arts have also played significant roles in political expression. In Chile, during the brutal dictatorship of Augusto Pinochet, women used arpilleras—patchwork pictures crafted from scraps of cloth—to depict the harsh realities of their lives and the disappearances of their loved ones. These textiles, often vibrant and poignant, were smuggled out of the country and sold internationally, bringing global attention to the human rights violations occurring in Chile. The act of sewing, typically dismissed as mere women's work, was transformed into a powerful act of political resistance and solidarity.

In more contemporary contexts, craftivism, a term coined in the early 21st century, combines craft and activism, where the process of creating is explicitly linked to political activism. This movement has been embraced by women worldwide, using crafts as a form of peaceful protest and advocacy on issues ranging from women's rights and environmental sustainability to anti-war movements. The Pussyhat Project, which began in 2017 in response to the inauguration of Donald Trump and aimed at addressing women's issues and promoting women's solidarity, saw thousands of women knitting pink cat-eared hats. These hats quickly became a symbol of resistance and were worn at Women's Marches across the globe, showcasing how traditional crafts can be mobilized for contemporary political purposes.

The sociopolitical impact of women's crafts is profound, highlighting the ways in which these practices are interwoven with the fabrics of historical and contemporary social movements. Women, through their crafts, have found unique voices in political dialogues, often in societies that otherwise marginalize their public and political expressions. These crafts are not only forms of personal and cultural expression but also acts of political resistance and empowerment, demonstrating the power of traditional women's work to influence, protest, and reshape the world.

ᐅᐅᐅ

"Women in music production master the art of sound, turning waves into symphonies of change and harmonies that heal the rifts within our society."

FIFTEEN

Muses in Motion: Celebrating Female Dance Revolutionaries

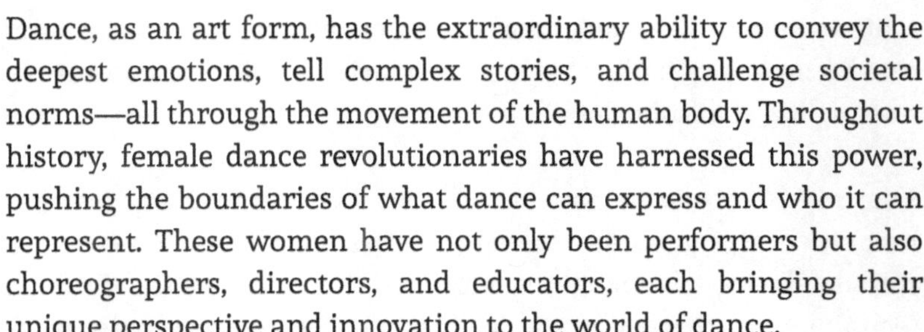

Dance, as an art form, has the extraordinary ability to convey the deepest emotions, tell complex stories, and challenge societal norms—all through the movement of the human body. Throughout history, female dance revolutionaries have harnessed this power, pushing the boundaries of what dance can express and who it can represent. These women have not only been performers but also choreographers, directors, and educators, each bringing their unique perspective and innovation to the world of dance.

From the ballrooms of early modern Europe to the contemporary stages of global theaters, women have been pivotal in evolving various dance forms and using dance as a platform for social change, artistic expression, and personal liberation. Their contributions have often disrupted traditional narratives and expanded the dance community's views on beauty, form, and the role of dance in society.

One of the earliest pioneers in the field of modern dance was Isadora Duncan, who in the early 20th century, broke away from the rigid structures of classical ballet and promoted a new form of free movement that emphasized naturalism and emotion over formal technique. Duncan's performances celebrated the human spirit and individualism, and her style was considered revolutionary. She draped her body in flowing tunics, dancing barefoot, and used her movements to express her personal and political beliefs, including her views on women's rights, the beauty of nature, and the importance of freedom. Duncan's legacy is foundational, as she laid the groundwork for what would become modern dance, influencing generations of dancers and choreographers.

In the realms of ballet, figures like Tamara Karsavina and Anna Pavlova emerged in the early 20th century, showcasing their prowess not only as iconic performers but also as innovators within the classical ballet genre. Pavlova, renowned for her performance in "The Dying Swan," infused the piece with such emotion and grace that it remains a benchmark for ballerinas worldwide. Her commitment to ballet helped popularize it across continents, making ballet a truly global art form.

The mid-20th century saw the rise of Martha Graham, another monumental figure in modern dance. Graham developed a completely new language of movement, known as the Graham technique, which used contraction and release as its basis. Her work dealt with complex themes such as human struggle, passion, and ecstasy, translating psychological and emotional depth into physical movement. Graham's influence is vast—she not only transformed American dance but also trained and inspired future generations of dancers and choreographers, including Merce Cunningham and Paul Taylor.

Another influential figure, Katherine Dunham, integrated African and Caribbean movements into American dance, creating a dynamic fusion that reflected her ethnographic research in these regions. Dunham was not just a choreographer but also an activist, using her dance company and school to challenge racial segregation and promote African American culture. Her legacy extends beyond her performances to her humanitarian work and her role in the civil rights movement.

The late 20th and early 21st centuries have seen contemporary female dancers and choreographers continue to innovate and inspire. Figures like Pina Bausch and Twyla Tharp have redefined what dance can be. Bausch's dance theater works are renowned for their emotional depth and stark, often brutal portrayal of human relationships. Her pieces frequently blur the lines between dance, theater, and reality, compelling audiences to confront their feelings and preconceptions. Twyla Tharp, known for her crossover ballets that incorporate both modern and jazz elements, has created works that are energetic, complex, and accessible, expanding the audience for contemporary dance.

These female dance revolutionaries have not only crafted exquisite performances but have also addressed issues such as gender stereotypes, racial injustice, and human rights through their art. Their work challenges and delights, disrupts, and redefines, continuing to influence both the dance community and the wider cultural landscape. The stories of these women are not just about the evolution of dance as an art form but also about the power of dance to move, to inspire, and to transform. As educators, innovators, and performers, they have each contributed uniquely to the narrative of dance, ensuring its vitality and relevance across generations.

ppp

"Through the threads of textiles, women weave the continuum of culture, each pattern a pulse of history, each fabric a flag of fortitude."

SIXTEEN

THE ART OF HEALING: WOMEN IN ART THERAPY

Art therapy, an interdisciplinary practice that bridges the fields of art and psychological healing, offers a unique approach to addressing emotional, cognitive, and developmental issues. Within this therapeutic context, women have been at the forefront, not only in practicing art therapy but also in shaping its theories and methodologies.

Their contributions have significantly enriched the field, bringing nuanced perspectives on the intersection of art, healing, and holistic health.

The roots of art therapy can be traced back to the mid-20th century, a period marked by burgeoning interest in alternative therapeutic methods. Women pioneers such as Margaret Naumburg and Edith Kramer were instrumental in establishing art therapy as a distinct discipline. Naumburg, often considered the "mother of art therapy," promoted the use of art as a spontaneous and cathartic expression, believing that the process of creating art could reveal subconscious thoughts and emotions similar to dreams.

Her approach emphasized the symbolic communication of feelings and conflicts through the art-making process, thereby offering insights that could be therapeutically beneficial.

Edith Kramer, another key figure in the early development of art therapy, approached the discipline with a slightly different emphasis. She saw art therapy not only as a diagnostic tool but as a therapeutic one that could help individuals manage their behaviors and emotions through the act of creation. Kramer's work particularly focused on children and adolescents, advocating for art as a means of sublimation and a channel for productive self-expression.

These foundational perspectives laid the groundwork for the broader application of art therapy across various settings, including hospitals, schools, community centers, and private practices. As the field grew, so did the diversity of its applications, with women continuing to lead and innovate.

Women art therapists expanded the practice into areas dealing with severe trauma, mental illness, and societal crises, tailoring art therapy techniques to help specific populations, including veterans, victims of abuse, and individuals with severe mental health issues.

For instance, Cathy Malchiodi, a contemporary leader in the field, has extensively explored the use of art therapy with trauma survivors, emphasizing its efficacy in non-verbal expression, which can often articulate what words cannot. Malchiodi's work highlights how art therapy provides a safe outlet for the expression of complex emotions associated with trauma, fostering healing and resilience.

Art therapy's versatility also extends to dealing with chronic illnesses and disabilities. Women art therapists have developed programs that address the psychological and emotional challenges associated with chronic health conditions, using art-making to improve patients' quality of life, enhance their coping strategies, and express their feelings about illness and treatment. These therapeutic strategies not only help alleviate symptoms but also empower individuals by validating their experiences and feelings.

Moreover, in the realm of mental health, art therapy has been particularly impactful in the treatment of depression, anxiety, and eating disorders, offering a therapeutic outlet for expression and self-reflection. Women art therapists have been at the forefront of using creative processes to help individuals explore their identities, improve self-esteem, and reduce distress.

The practice of art therapy by women extends beyond individual therapy sessions to community and social activism. Many women art therapists use community-based art therapy programs to address broader social issues, such as community trauma, social exclusion, and intergenerational conflicts.

These programs often involve collaborative art projects that not only aid in healing individual participants but also foster community solidarity and understanding.

The influence of women in art therapy is also evident in academic and research spheres. Female academics in this field have contributed extensively to the body of research that supports art therapy as a legitimate and effective therapeutic practice. Through rigorous studies and publications, they continue to advocate for art therapy's integration into mainstream healthcare practices and public health policies.

Women's involvement in art therapy reflects a broader commitment to nurturing the connection between creativity and healing. Their work in the field has not only provided therapeutic benefits to individuals and communities but also highlighted the profound impact of the arts in fostering holistic well-being.

As art therapy continues to evolve, the pioneering efforts of these women ensure that it remains a compassionate, innovative, and inclusive practice, dedicated to healing and transformation at both individual and societal levels.

ᐯᐯᐯ

"The stages managed by women in theatre are not merely platforms; they are canvases where life's deepest dramas unfold, painted with the hues of human emotion."

SEVENTEEN

BREAKING BOUNDARIES: WOMEN IN EXPERIMENTAL ARTS

The world of experimental arts has always been a fertile ground for pushing the boundaries of traditional aesthetics and conceptual frameworks. Within this avant-garde realm, women artists have played a critical role, often using their work to challenge conventions and explore new possibilities in art-making. Their contributions to experimental arts span across disciplines, including performance, multimedia, installation, and digital arts, effectively redefining what art can be and what it can achieve in terms of both form and content.

Historically, women in experimental arts have often operated on the margins of the art world, where they found the freedom to explore radical ideas and expressive forms. Despite facing significant obstacles, including institutional discrimination and limited access to resources, these women have not only persisted but also thrived, crafting works that offer profound insights into social, political, and personal themes.

One of the early pioneers in the field of experimental arts was Gertrude Stein. As a writer and art patron, Stein's non-linear prose and her role in the Parisian avant-garde scene of the early 20th century helped shape modernist literature and influenced many experimental artists who followed. Her salon was a gathering place for key figures of modernism, providing a space where artists and writers could exchange ideas that challenged traditional narratives nd forms.

In the visual arts, figures such as Louise Bourgeois and Yoko Ono have been instrumental in expanding the parameters of artistic expression. Bourgeois's work, which spans six decades, explores themes of domesticity, family, sexuality, and the body, often through large-scale sculptures and installations that incorporate diverse materials and forms. Her deeply personal approach to art-making has opened up new pathways for emotional and psychological exploration in art.

Yoko Ono, a multimedia artist and peace activist, has been a significant figure in the experimental art scene since the 1960s. Her performance pieces, installations, and conceptual art projects often require viewer participation and challenge the passive consumption of art. Ono's "Cut Piece," a performance where she invited audience members to cut pieces from her clothing, poignantly addresses themes of vulnerability, trust, and materiality, pushing the boundaries of performance art and its potential for social commentary.

In more recent decades, the advent of digital technology has provided new tools and mediums for experimental artists. Women like Lynn Hershman Leeson have embraced these technologies, using them to explore the intersections of art and artificial intelligence, biotechnology, and issues of surveillance and privacy.

Hershman Leeson's work is often interactive, inviting engagement from viewers to complete the work or reveal deeper layers of meaning, thereby redefining the relationship between art, artist, and audience.

The experimental art of today also sees significant contributions from women working in less traditional mediums, such as sound and light. Artists like Olafur Eliasson and Janet Cardiff utilize these elements to create immersive environments that alter perceptions and engage the senses in unconventional ways. Their work challenges the traditional confines of the gallery space and invites viewers to experience art through more than just visual observation, promoting a holistic encounter that can be both disorienting and enlightening.

Furthermore, women in experimental arts often use their work to address critical social and political issues. Kara Walker's silhouetted figures, which often play out disturbing scenes of racial and historical violence, challenge the viewer to reconsider history and its impact on contemporary society. Her bold approach to subject matter and scale makes her work a powerful commentary on identity and power dynamics.

Women's contributions to experimental arts are thus characterized by a relentless questioning of the status quo and a continuous exploration of new artistic territories. Their work not only expands the scope of what art can encompass but also deepens our understanding of the myriad ways in which art interacts with and influences society. By breaking boundaries in their artistic expressions, these women not only pave the way for future generations of artists but also ensure that the experimental arts remain a dynamic and critical field of human creativity.

ᗐᗐᗐ

"Each pot shaped by the hands of women potters contains more than earth; it holds stories, sustains spirits, and pours out the heritage of hearts hardened by fire."

EIGHTEEN

ECHOES OF THE ANCESTORS: INDIGENOUS WOMEN ARTISTS

Indigenous women artists play a crucial role in preserving and revitalizing the cultural heritage of their communities, intertwining the echoes of their ancestors with contemporary expressions and narratives. Their art transcends mere aesthetics, functioning as a dynamic repository of tradition, a form of resistance against cultural erasure, and a declaration of identity and sovereignty. These artists harness various mediums—from painting and sculpture to textiles and digital media—to communicate stories, beliefs, and histories that are often marginalized in mainstream cultural discourses.

The work of indigenous women artists is deeply embedded in the contexts of their specific cultural backgrounds and experiences. It reflects a continuum of tradition, where ancient motifs, techniques, and themes are interwoven with contemporary issues and personal expressions. These artists not only maintain the artistic traditions passed down through generations but also adapt them to speak to current realities, such as environmental challenges, social injustices, and the struggles for rights and recognition.

A profound example of this artistic tradition can be seen in the work of Jaune Quick-to-See Smith, a Flathead Salish artist whose paintings and collages critique the ongoing impacts of colonization on Native American communities. Smith combines abstract expressionism with symbolic elements drawn from Native American visual culture, creating layered works that critique contemporary social issues while celebrating indigenous heritage. Her use of collage, incorporating newsprint and imagery from popular culture, serves as a powerful commentary on the commodification and misrepresentation of Native American cultures.

Similarly, in Australia, Aboriginal women artists have been at the forefront of a movement to revive and sustain traditional artistic practices. Artists like Emily Kame Kngwarreye, who started painting in her late 70s, brought international attention to the rich visual language of the Utopia community in the Northern Territory. Her work, characterized by vibrant color fields and intricate dotting techniques, is deeply connected to the Dreamtime stories and landscapes of her community. Kngwarreye's paintings are not merely aesthetic objects but are imbued with cultural and spiritual significances, serving as visual manifestations of her connection to the land and ancestral heritage.

In the Arctic regions, Inuit women artists like Kenojuak Ashevak have gained acclaim for their distinctive printmaking and sculpture. Ashevak's art is renowned for its vivid depictions of Arctic wildlife and mythology, rendered in a style that is both whimsical and profound. Her work reflects the symbiotic relationship between the Inuit people and their harsh, beautiful environment, capturing the spirituality and resilience inherent in her culture. Through her artistic achievements, Ashevak has played a key role in introducing Inuit art to the world, thereby fostering a greater appreciation for its unique beauty and cultural depth.

Textiles and weaving hold a special place in indigenous cultures around the world, often associated with women's knowledge and community roles. In many indigenous communities, women weavers are considered keepers of cultural secrets, encoding histories, myths, and cultural knowledge into their textiles. For instance, Maya women in Guatemala use backstrap loom weaving to produce textiles that are both functional and richly symbolic. These textiles often feature complex patterns and colors that narrate stories of the Mayan cosmology, community life, and the natural world. Through their weaving, these women maintain a tangible connection to their ancestors, while also adapting their creations to reflect contemporary life and challenges.

Indigenous women artists also use their art as a tool for education and cultural preservation, teaching younger generations the skills and knowledge that ensure the survival of their artistic traditions. This educational role is crucial, especially in communities where indigenous languages and practices are endangered. By passing on their artistic knowledge, these women ensure that the essence of their culture is not lost to time but evolves and adapts in the hands of new generations.

Moreover, the global reach of indigenous art today challenges stereotypes and invites international audiences to understand the complexity and diversity of indigenous cultures. Indigenous women artists, through exhibitions, collaborations, and digital media, engage in dialogues that cross cultural boundaries, promoting a deeper understanding of indigenous worldviews and issues.

In conclusion, the art of indigenous women is a vibrant expression of resilience, a celebration of continuity, and a profound act of cultural affirmation. These artists are not merely preserving traditions; they are actively reimagining and revitalizing their cultural legacies in a globalized world. Their work serves as a bridge between past and present, personal and collective, offering not only a visual feast but also a deep, resonant voice in the global cultural conversation.

ΡΡΡ

"Women's contributions to the arts are like rivers—constantly flowing, reshaping landscapes, and nourishing the fields of creativity that lie in their wake."

NINETEEN

FUTURE VISIONS: EMERGING WOMEN ARTISTS TO WATCH

The landscape of contemporary art is perpetually evolving, marked by the emergence of new voices and visions that challenge conventional boundaries and introduce fresh perspectives. Among these transformative forces are numerous emerging women artists whose innovative works not only captivate audiences but also provoke thought, inspire change, and reimagine the future of art. These artists, diverse in their approaches and backgrounds, explore a range of themes from identity and social justice to technology and environmentalism, marking them as significant contributors to the global art scene.

One of the defining characteristics of these emerging artists is their fearless experimentation with mediums and forms. Whether through digital art, installations, performance, or traditional painting and sculpture, these women are not afraid to push the boundaries of what art can be and what it can achieve. Their work often reflects a deep engagement with current issues, making art not only a form of expression but also a tool of social commentary and a space for critical inquiry.

A poignant example of this trend is the work of Firelei Báez, a Dominican-American artist known for her intricate works on paper and large-scale installations. Báez's work explores the intricacies of cultural identity, migration, and the historical narratives of the African diaspora. Her use of lush, colorful imagery drawn from folklore and tradition serves as a powerful visual narrative that reclaims the stories of marginalized communities. Báez's work is a celebration of resilience and a testament to the power of art to traverse cultural boundaries.

Another artist making significant waves is Toyin Ojih Odutola, a Nigerian-American artist whose detailed pen-and-ink drawings challenge conventional notions of identity and skin color. Odutola creates intricate, textured portraits that explore the sociopolitical constructs of race and diversity. Her portraits are not just representations of individuals; they are profound explorations of the complexities of skin as a landscape that carries depth, history, and nuanced stories of colorism and identity.

In the realm of performance art, Ana Prvački, through her engaging and often humorous installations and performances, invites viewers to reconsider the mundane aspects of everyday life and their interactions with the environment around them. Her work, which often incorporates elements of etiquette, communication, and environmental consciousness, encourages a mindfulness in personal and collective practices, suggesting subtle yet impactful ways to improve communal life and relationships.

Emerging women artists are also at the forefront of technological integration in art. Artists like Refik Anadol, who work with data and machine learning to create immersive installations, represent a new wave of digital artists whose practices redefine the viewer's interaction with art. Anadol's work, often large-scale and visually mesmerizing, utilizes collected data to create dynamic visualizations that transform spaces and create a dialogue between the digital and physical worlds.

Environmental concerns are another critical area addressed by contemporary women artists. Olafur Eliasson, for example, uses natural elements and scientific principles to create large-scale installations that highlight the urgency of climate change. Her works are experiential, crafted to evoke emotional and intellectual responses from viewers, prompting them to think critically about their relationship with the natural world and their role in its preservation.

These emerging artists contribute to a vibrant, dynamic global art scene that reflects a broad spectrum of experiences, perspectives, and challenges. Their work often transcends the aesthetic, offering new ways of understanding and interacting with the world. Through their diverse practices, they challenge audiences to reconsider established norms and to imagine new possibilities for the future of art and society.

As the art world continues to evolve, the influence of these emerging women artists is increasingly significant. They not only bring fresh perspectives and innovations to the field but also ensure that the art world remains a relevant, responsive, and inclusive space. Their voices and visions, rich in narrative and complexity, promise to shape the contours of contemporary art for years to come, making them truly artists to watch.

ppp

"In the silence of studios, women composers orchestrate the soundtracks of our existence, their scores a symphony of the soul that speaks without words."

TWENTY

CELEBRATING SILENCE AND SOUND: WOMEN IN THE WORLD OF MUSIC PRODUCTION

The world of music production, traditionally dominated by men, has seen a transformative influx of talented women who are redefining the industry's landscape through their innovative work. Women in music production are not only changing the sounds that resonate from our speakers; they are challenging the industry norms, advocating for diversity, and creating new spaces for creative expression. Their contributions span across genres and roles—from sound engineering to mixing, mastering, and producing—each adding a distinct touch that enhances the richness of the music industry.

The importance of recognizing women in music production cannot be overstated, as their presence and success directly challenge the gender disparities that have long characterized this field. Historically, the technical aspects of music, particularly production and sound engineering, have been areas where women have faced significant barriers to entry, including lack of mentorship, gender bias, and unequal opportunities for advancement.

Despite these challenges, numerous women have risen to prominence and are pioneering change. Sylvia Massy, for instance, is a renowned producer and engineer known for her work with legends such as Prince, Johnny Cash, and Tool. Massy's unconventional techniques and bold approach to sound recording have earned her a reputation as one of the most innovative minds in the business.

Her willingness to experiment with different recording setups and her fearless manipulation of sound textures have resulted in some of the most iconic sounds in rock and alternative music.

Another influential figure in the industry is Linda Perry, a former lead singer who transitioned into a successful career in music production. Perry's work with artists like P!nk, Christina Aguilera, and Gwen Stefani has been pivotal in shaping their careers, helping them forge distinctive sonic identities.

As a producer, Perry is known for her ability to connect deeply with artists, nurturing their creative talents and encouraging them to explore new musical territories. Her advocacy for artist authenticity and her hands-on approach in the studio have helped craft some of the biggest hits in pop music.

The electronic music scene has also seen groundbreaking contributions from women like Imogen Heap, who merges her classical music training with innovative technology to create unique soundscapes. Heap's use of the Mi.Mu gloves, which allow her to manipulate sound through hand gestures, exemplifies her pioneering approach to music production and performance.

This technology not only enhances her musical expression but also pushes the boundaries of how technology and music interact, making her performances a captivating blend of artistry and invention.

In recent years, the rise of digital audio workstations (DAW) and home recording technologies has democratized music production, providing more women with the tools to create and produce music independently. Artists like Grimes have taken full advantage of these technologies, producing their own music and thereby maintaining creative control over their work.

Grimes's approach to music production—incorporating elements of pop, electronica, and experimental music—highlights her versatility and skill as a producer and challenges the traditional perceptions of women's roles in music technology.

Moreover, women in music production are not only influencing the sound and production techniques but are also leading efforts to address the industry's gender disparities. Initiatives and organizations such as Women's Audio Mission (WAM) and SoundGirls are dedicated to supporting women in audio through education, community building, and advocacy, aiming to increase the representation of women in the field. These organizations provide crucial support networks, training, and resources that help aspiring women producers and engineers navigate the challenges of the industry.

Celebrating women in music production involves acknowledging their contributions to the sonic landscapes that define contemporary music and recognizing their roles in mentoring the next generation of female producers. Their work challenges the industry's status quo and paves the way for a more inclusive and diverse musical future.

Through their creativity, resilience, and innovation, these women are not just making music; they are shaping the future of sound.

ᕤᕤᕤ

"In every pixel and frame of animation crafted by women, there lies a universe of potential, a canvas for revolution, and a storyboard for tomorrow."

TWENTY-ONE
SUMMARY

The tapestry of women's contributions to the arts, explored in detail throughout this volume, tells a compelling story of resilience, innovation, and transformation. Spanning various disciplines and eras, from the ancient echoes of women potters to the digital revolutions instigated by contemporary female artists, this narrative reveals the profound impact women have had on shaping the cultural and artistic landscapes across the globe. The concluding chapter aims to weave together these diverse threads, providing a panoramic view of the artistic milestones achieved by women and reflecting on the persistent challenges they face.

The journey begins with the pioneers of paint, early women who marked the canvases of history with their rich contributions despite societal restrictions. Artists like Artemisia Gentileschi and Mary Cassatt didn't merely paint; they challenged the very narratives and representations of women in art, asserting a powerful presence in a male-dominated field. Their legacies, characterized by bold strokes and poignant portrayals, laid the groundwork for generations of women to pursue and excel in the visual arts.

In the realm of performance, women choreographers like Martha Graham and Pina Bausch revolutionized the dance world by introducing novel concepts and expressive techniques that delved deep into human emotions and societal issues. Their work not only transformed how dance was perceived and what it could communicate but also paved the way for women to assume leadership roles in choreography and dance production, historically male-dominated arenas.

Sculpture and public art, too, felt the imprint of female creativity, with artists like Louise Bourgeois and Maya Lin using space and form to explore complex themes such as identity, memory, and loss. These women extended the boundaries of sculpture, moving it beyond traditional forms and materials to engage with viewers in more interactive, contemplative, and often challenging ways.

The narrative then shifts to the auditory realm, where women in music production have carved out sonic landscapes that resonate with innovation and diversity. Figures like Sylvia Massy and Missy Elliott have not only crafted hits but have also disrupted the typical sound engineering and production paradigms, advocating for more inclusive and representative music industry practices.

In literature, women have wielded the pen with equal might, using narrative to challenge societal norms and articulate the female experience in all its complexity. Authors like Virginia Woolf and Toni Morrison crafted stories that explored the depths of female consciousness and societal structures, inspiring readers and writers to consider the nuances of gender, race, and historical context in their engagements with literature.

Emerging technologies have also seen significant contributions from women, particularly in digital arts and animation. Artists like Lynn Hershman Leeson have explored the intersections of art and technology, pushing the boundaries of what digital media can achieve and how it can be experienced by audiences. This exploration is mirrored in the growing field of art therapy, where women have used the creative process as a tool for healing and psychological exploration, highlighting art's profound impact on personal and communal healing.

The environmental and sociopolitical realms have not been untouched by the artistic endeavors of women. Through crafts and community art projects, women have addressed global issues of environmental degradation, social injustice, and community cohesion, using art as a platform for activism and change.

As this volume demonstrates, the contributions of women to the arts are not merely about filling gaps in the historical record. They represent a continuous, dynamic force that challenges, reshapes, and enriches the global cultural heritage. The stories of these women are not just narratives of overcoming but are also visions of what is possible when creativity is combined with courage and resilience.

In summary, the arts provide a reflective surface for the progress and ongoing struggles of women across all societies. The achievements highlighted in this book are testaments to the enduring spirit and transformative power of women in the arts. As we look to the future, it is clear that the journey of women in the arts is far from complete. The challenge now is to build on this rich heritage, ensuring that women's voices are amplified and their work celebrated, not just as a separate category but as an integral and invaluable part of the global artistic canon.

ᗡᗡᗡ

Citation And References

This book represents the culmination of extensive research and meticulous analysis, incorporating a diverse range of sources, including numerous books, scholarly studies, and personal experiences. Additionally, I have scoured various websites to gather relevant information and data essential for the compilation of this work. I have taken every precaution to ensure the accuracy of the information presented and have diligently cited all sources to acknowledge their contributions.

Despite these efforts, the possibility of inadvertent errors remains. I deeply value the insights of my readers and appreciate any feedback that can help identify and rectify such inaccuracies. I encourage you to bring any discrepancies to my attention.

Your feedback is not only welcome but crucial, as it will aid in correcting current editions and enhancing the content of future ones. I am committed to maintaining the highest standards of accuracy and reliability in my work and thank you for your support and understanding.

Additionally, I firmly uphold the principle of freedom of speech and expression as guaranteed under Article 19(1)(a) of the Constitution of India, and I respect the diverse viewpoints and expressions of all readers.

ppp

Other Books Of The Author

1. Empowering Minds: A Journey into Women's Self-Discovery and Power
2. The Dynamics of Motivation: Catalyzing Thought into Action
3. Meditation and Mental Well Being: The Path to Inner Peace and Clarity
4. The Psychology of Child Education: Nurturing Future Generations
5. Ethical Enlightenment: A Modern Guide to Living with Integrity
6. Voices of Empowerment: Stories of Women Rising Against Odds
7. Social Psychology in Everyday Life: Understanding Human Connections
8. The Essence of Motivational Speaking: Inspiring Change in Others
9. Balancing Acts: Women, Work, and the Will to Lead
10. Guiding with Grace: Raising Children with Compassion and Awareness
11. The Power of Positive Aging: Embracing Life After Fifty
12. Building Resilient Communities: Social Work in Action
13. The Ethical Educator: Principles for Teaching and Learning
14. From Insight to Impact: Social Psychology for a Better World
15. The Ethics of Empathy: A Guide to Ethical Living
16. The Science of Empowering the Self: Navigating Life's Challenges with Psychological Wisdom
17. The Mindful Conscious Leader: Meditation Techniques for Modern Management
18. Pioneering Spirit: Women's Pathways to Leadership and Empowerment
19. Feeling to Healing: The Role of Emotional Intelligence in Child Development
20. Transformative Talks and Words of Inspiration: Insights into Motivational Oratory

21. Green Ethics: A Path to Sustainable Living
22. Spiritual Integrity: Navigating Life with Moral Compassion
23. Clean Living, Clean Society: The Ethics of Cleanliness
24. Patriotic Spirits: Building a Nation on Positive Attitudes
25. Innovative Integrity & Vibrant Visions: The Ethical and Entrepreneurial Spirit of Gujarat
26. Youthful Visions, Endless Possibilities: Inspiring Ethics and Motivation in Children
27. Living Your Legacy: How to Motivate Others by Living Your Values
28. Secret of Healing Conversations: Ethical Practices in Counselling and Therapy
29. Creative Kindness: Crafting a Life of Compassion and Creativity
30. The Power of Appreciation: How Gratitude Can Transform Your Relationships
31. Bhagavad-Gita: Messages
32. Science of Art: The New Frontier of Fashion Modernism
33. Vivekananda's Virtues: A Blueprint for Modern Living
34. Empower Her: Navigating the Path to Women's Entrepreneurship
35. The Boundless Classroom: Innovations in Global Education
36. The Language of Leadership: Communicating with Authenticity and Impact
37. The Warrior's Mantra: Deciphering the Hanuman Chalisa
38. Echoes of Empathy: Transformative Stories of Social Service
39. Artful Living: Cultivating Creativity in Your Daily Routine
40. Finding Your Why: Discovering Your Passions and Charting Your Course
41. The Role of Social Media in Shaping Self-Esteem and Interpersonal Relationships among Adolescents
42. Karma's Tapestry: Weaving a Life of Selfless Service
43. Altruistic Alchemy: Transforming Lives Through Giving
44. The Blueprint of Pro-Activeness and Productivity: Crafting Habits for Success
45. The Simplicity with Grounded Wisdom: Embracing Authenticity

Bhajan
101. Pilgrimage of the Soul: Spiritual Journeys in India

❧❧❧

Contact

Dr. Minakshi Bansal
Social Activist
Ahmedabad, Gujarat, Bharat
minakshiindiag20@yahoo.com

❦❦❦

|| LOKAHA SAMASTHAHA SUKHINO BHAVANTU ||